# I Love Being

**April Allen**

*Illustrations by:*
*Eldon Jones III*

Halo
Publishing International

ISBN 13: 978-1-61244-507-6
Library of Congress Control Number: 2016915381

Printed in the United States of America

Halo
Publishing International
www.halopublishing.com

Published by Halo Publishing International
1100 NW Loop 410
Suite 700 - 176
San Antonio, Texas 78213
Toll Free 1-877-705-9647
www.halopublishing.com
www.holapublishing.com
e-mail: contact@halopublishing.com

To my adoring husband, who loves me being me.  To my Cupcake, Ella, and Gummy Bear, Chloe, my prayer is that you see your own unique beauty and love being who you were created to be.

Hi! My name is Liberty Belle Allen, but you can call me Libby for short, and I love being me.

I love being me.  I love being me because that is who I was created to be.

My big curly hair is everywhere. I don't care if you stare because I love my hair, and I love being me.

I dance and laugh because I am free.  I look in the mirror and like what I see because I love being me.

Now, I must tell you that I love many things.

I love running, jumping high, and eating pizza and cake.
I even love skateboarding and to ice skate.

I love the park and going high on the swings.
I love listening to music and to dance and sing.

I love riding on airplanes and seeing animals at the zoo.

I also love wearing princess dresses with one pink and one blue tennis shoe.

But above all these things, I adore even more being me because I truly love being me.

I love being me. I love being me because that is who I was created to be.

I also love my friends and how different they are.
Each one is like a special, gigantic star.

I love my friend, Lindsey, who likes telling jokes and having fun.  Her hair is gold like the color of the sun. When we are together, we always laugh a ton.

I also love my friend, Christine, whose hair is black. She likes wearing it in a braid going down her back.  Christine's hair is so long, when we play hide and seek, she hides her hair under her feet.

I love my friend, Emma, who is as sweet as they come. When her mom makes chocolate chip cookies, she always brings me some. Emma's hair is curly and the color of cherries, apples, and my favorite fruit, strawberries.

I love my friend, Catalina, whose hair is brown like a lion's mane. Sometimes she wears it in a ponytail when we are playing outside, and it's pouring down rain.

I love playing with my friends, Shannon, Mandy, and Carrie Grace, who love pretending to be astronauts and reading books about traveling to outer space. When it's hot outside, we all wear long braids and go swimming together pretending to be beautiful mermaids.

One of the friends I love the most is Rena.  When we are together, we put our curly hair in buns, wear tutus, and spin around like ballerinas.

I also love my friend, Rashini, whose hair is black highlighted with pink. When we are together, she likes to do science experiments that make us really think.

As you can see, my friends and I are all beautiful and different as can be.  My friends love being who they are, and I love them, but I still love being me.

I don't want to look or be any other way.  We all look differently, and that makes me say hooray!

I love being me.  I love being me because I was made to be who I am supposed to be.  From my hair down to my feet, I was created perfectly, so I love being me.

Simply put, I am so happy and free because I love, love, love being me!

Dear Dad, Mom, and/or Loved One,

My deepest wish in writing this book is that
every little girl understands that her uniqueness makes
her special and beautiful.  I want your daughter, niece,
granddaughter, god-daughter or little friend to understand that
we are not all meant to look and act the same.  We are meant
to be different as that is what makes us truly one of a kind and
irreplaceable.  I want her to love being her.  My second hope
in writing this book is that girls are taught to create their
own standard of beauty and to help them understand beauty
comes in all skin and hair colors, hair textures and lengths, and
all shapes and sizes.  All beauty deserves to be appreciated and
celebrated even if different than yours.  Most importantly, I hope
us adults teach our girls that true and lasting beauty comes from
how we love ourselves and love others.

With Love,
April Allen

CPSIA information can be obtained
at www.ICGtesting.com
Printed in the USA
BVOW05s1045060717
488631BV00005B/8/P